TIPS TO SUPPORT LITERACY AT HOME

WHY READING AND SINGING WITH YOUR CHILD IS SO IMPORTANT

Daily reading with your child leads to increased academic achievement. Music and songs, specifically rhyming songs, are a fun and easy way to build early literacy and language development. Music skills correlate significantly with both phonological awareness and reading development. Singing helps build vocabulary and speech development. And reading and appreciating music together is a wonderful way to strengthen your relationship.

READ AND SING EVERY DAY!

TIPS FOR USING CANTATA LEARNING BOOKS AND SONGS DURING YOUR DAILY STORY TIME

1. As you sing and read, point out the different words on the page that rhyme. Suggest other words that rhyme.

2. Memorize simple rhymes such as Itsy Bitsy Spider and sing them together. This encourages comprehension skills and early literacy skills.

3. Use the questions in the back of each book to guide your singing and storytelling.

4. Read the included sheet music with your child while you listen to the song. How do the music notes correlate to the words of the song?

5. Sing along on the go and at home. Access music by scanning the QR code on each Cantata book. You can also stream or download the music for free to your computer, smartphone, or mobile device.

Devoting time to daily reading shows that you are available for your child. Together, you are building language, literacy, and listening skills.

Have fun reading and singing!

Time is a way of measuring our world, and clocks measure time. **Analog** clocks have faces with numbers around the edges. A short pointer, or hand, tells the hour. A long hand tells the minute. **Digital** clocks have a screen with numbers on it. The first number tells the hour. The second number tells the minutes.

No matter what kind of clock we look at, time is always the same. Hours are always sixty minutes long. Days always have twenty-four hours. Daytime always follows night. And nighttime always comes after day. Let's sing about telling time together!

At seven **o'clock** in the morning
we get up right away.
We dress and eat and go to school.
The bell will ring at eight.

At nine o'clock we're working hard.
We go to gym at ten.
We eat lunch at twelve, or **noon**,
when the hands line up again.

Every sixty minutes
one hour passes by.

Where's the short hand?
Where's the long hand?
Now we're telling time!

At three o'clock we finish school.

Where should the clock hands be?

The long hand points straight up at twelve.

The short hand points to three.

At four o'clock we're home again.
We have schoolwork or play.
At five it's almost time to eat.
We put our toys away.

Every sixty minutes
one hour passes by.

Where's the short hand?
Where's the long hand?
Now we're telling time!

At five **thirty** it's dinnertime.
What will the clock hands show?

The short hand is halfway from five to six.
The long hand points straight down.

Every thirty minutes half an hour passes by.
So halfway through the hour,
  we say "thirty" when telling time.

Every sixty minutes
one hour passes by.

Where's the short hand?
Where's the long hand?
Now we're telling time!

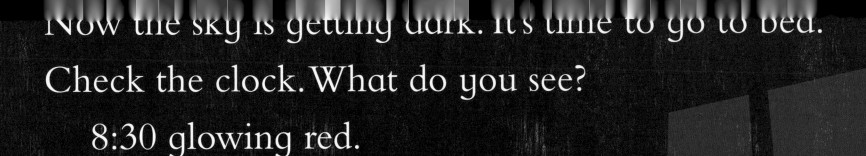

Now the sky is getting dark. It's time to go to bed.
Check the clock. What do you see?

8:30 glowing red.

As you dream, the hours tick by.
At nine and ten it's late.
Eleven o'clock at night is dark.
Midnight starts a new day.

Every sixty minutes
one hour passes by.

Where's the short hand?
Where's the long hand?
Now we're telling time!

SONG LYRICS
Telling Time

At seven o'clock in the morning we get up right away.
We dress and eat and go to school.
    The bell will ring at eight.

At nine o'clock we're working hard.
    We go to gym at ten.
We eat lunch at twelve, or noon,
    when the hands line up again.

Every sixty minutes
one hour passes by.
Where's the short hand?
Where's the long hand?
Now we're telling time!

At three o'clock we finish school.
    Where should the clock hands be?
The long hand points straight up at twelve.
    The short hand points to three.

At four o'clock we're home again.
    We have schoolwork or play.
At five it's almost time to eat. We put our toys away.

Every sixty minutes
one hour passes by.
Where's the short hand?
Where's the long hand?
Now we're telling time!

At five thirty it's dinnertime.
What will the clock hands show?
The short hand is halfway from five to six.
The long hand points straight down.

Every thirty minutes half an hour passes by.
So halfway through the hour,
    we say "thirty" when telling time.

Every sixty minutes
one hour passes by.
Where's the short hand?
Where's the long hand?
Now we're telling time!

Now the sky is getting dark. It's time to go to bed.
Check the clock. What do you see? 8:30 glowing red.

As you dream, the hours tick by.
    At nine and ten it's late.
Eleven o'clock at night is dark.
    Midnight starts a new day.

Every sixty minutes
one hour passes by.
Where's the short hand?
Where's the long hand?
Now we're telling time!